LINES, SEGMENTS, RAYS, AND ANGLES

Claire Piddock

Crabtree Publishing Company
www.crabtreebooks.com

Author: Claire Piddock
Publishing plan research and development:
  Sean Charlebois, Reagan Miller
  Crabtree Publishing Company
Editor: Molly Aloian
Editorial director: Kathy Middleton
Project coordinator: Margaret Salter
Prepress technician: Margaret Salter
Coordinating editor: Chester Fisher
Series editor: Jessica Cohn
Project manager: Kumar Kunal (Q2AMEDIA)
Art direction: Rahul Dhiman (Q2AMEDIA)
Cover design: Shruti Aggarwal (Q2AMEDIA)
Design: Shruti Aggarwal (Q2AMEDIA)
Photo research: Dimple Bhorwal (Q2AMEDIA)

Photographs:
Bigstockphoto: Marlene: p. 13
Corbis: Lester Lefkowitz: p. 19
Masterfile: p. 7
Photostogo: p. 5
Q2AMedia Art Bank : p. 3, p. 4, p. 6, p. 8, p. 10, p. 12, p. 14,
  p. 15 (bottom), p. 20, p. 21, p. 23
Shuttersock: Dan Tataru: front cover; Lori Martin: front cover (inset);
  Alexsol: title page; Monassevitch Elisheva: p. 4; Buchan: p. 9;
  June Marie Sobrito: p. 11; Racheal Grazias: p. 15 (top); Sharon
  Morris: p. 17

Library and Archives Canada Cataloguing in Publication

Piddock, Claire
  Lines, segments, rays and angles / Claire Piddock.

(My path to math)
Includes index.
ISBN 978-0-7787-5245-5 (bound).--ISBN 978-0-7787-5292-9 (pbk.)

  1. Angles (Geometry)--Juvenile literature. 2. Line geometry--Juvenile
literature. I. Title. II. Series: My path to math

QA482.P53 2009   j516   C2009-905421-3

Library of Congress Cataloging-in-Publication Data

Piddock, Claire.
  Lines, Segments, Rays, and Angles / Claire Piddock.
    p. cm. -- (My path to math)
  Includes index.
  ISBN 978-0-7787-5245-5 (reinforced lib. bdg. : alk. paper) -- ISBN 978-0-7787-
5292-9 (pbk. : alk. paper)
  1. Angles (Geometry)--Juvenile literature. 2. Line geometry--Juvenile
literature. I. Title. II. Series.

QA482.P53 2010
516--dc22
                                                    2009036008

Crabtree Publishing Company

www.crabtreebooks.com   1-800-387-7650

Printed in China/122009/CT20090903

Published in Canada
Crabtree Publishing
616 Welland Ave.
St. Catharines, ON
L2M 5V6

Published in the United States
Crabtree Publishing
PMB 59051
350 Fifth Avenue, 59th Floor
New York, New York 10118

Published in the United Kingdom
Crabtree Publishing
Maritime House
Basin Road North, Hove
BN41 1WR

Published in Australia
Crabtree Publishing
386 Mt. Alexander Rd.
Ascot Vale (Melbourne)
VIC 3032

Contents

Country Fair

The country fair is open! Signs for the fair are all over town. Grace and Ethan are going with their Aunt Sarah. It is an exciting day—filled with **geometry**! Geometry is the study of **points**, **lines**, and other shapes.

A point is an exact position. A line is a straight path that goes in both directions with no end.

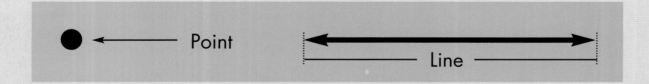

Point

Line

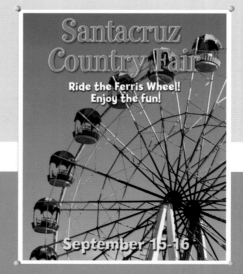

Activity Box

Look at the sign for the fair.
Find the four points.

Grace and Ethan are going to the fair with Aunt Sarah.

On the Way

On the way to the fair, they make a game of looking for lines. A telephone wire looks like a line!

Aunt Sarah explains the difference between a line and a **line segment**. A line segment is part of a line. It has points on each end called **endpoints**. A line has no endpoints.

The fence posts look like line segments.

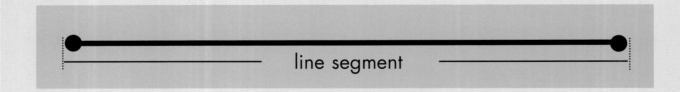
line segment

Activity Box

Use a pencil and a ruler to draw a line segment on a piece of paper.

line

line segment

Where else do you see lines
and line segments in the picture?

Rays

The fair has a ferris wheel. Ethan says that the spot in the middle is a point. Grace says that the spokes of the ferris wheel look like line segments.

Aunt Sarah says that they are both right. She then explains a geometry idea called a **ray**. She tells them to imagine a spoke of the ferris wheel going out in one direction with no end. That is a ray. The center of the wheel is the ray's endpoint.

A line continues on in both directions. A ray continues on in only one direction. A ray has one endpoint.

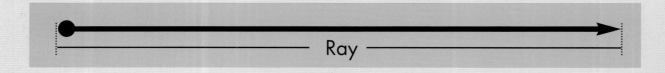

Ray

Activity Box

Think about the rays of the Sun.
How is a ray of sunlight like a ray?

Imagine the spokes of the ferris wheel as rays. What other kinds of wheels have spokes like rays?

Ray

Line segment

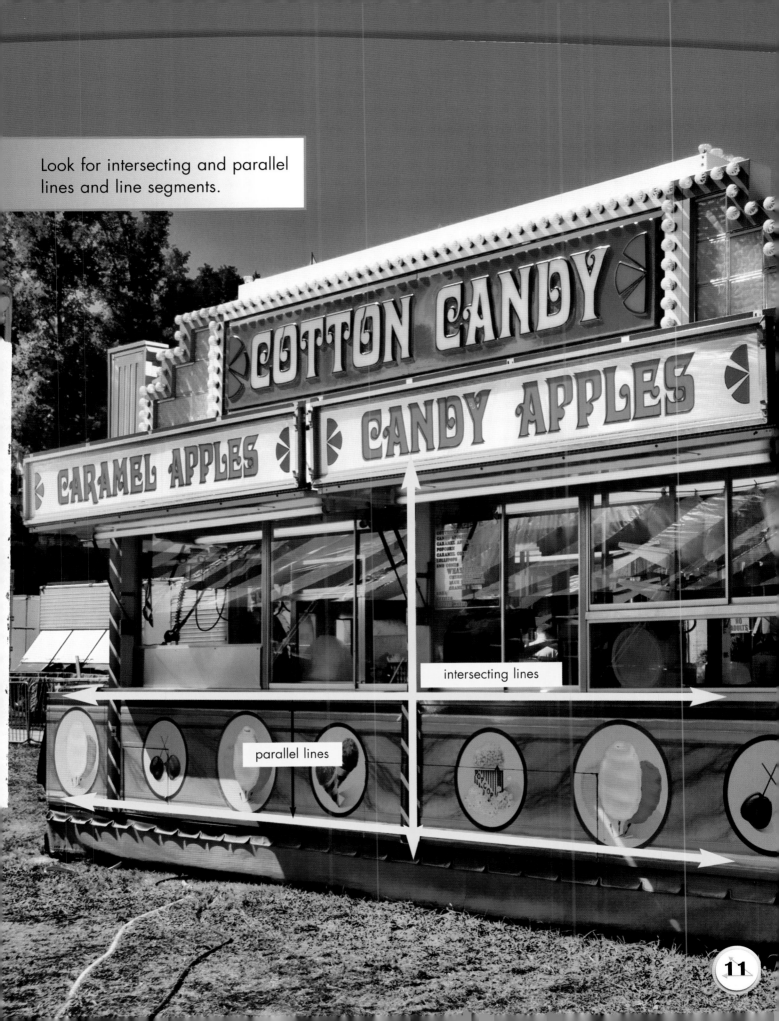

Look for intersecting and parallel lines and line segments.

COTTON CANDY

CANDY APPLES

CARAMEL APPLES

intersecting lines

parallel lines

Perpendicular Lines

At the carousel, Aunt Sarah points to the **perpendicular** lines.

Perpendicular lines cross in a special way. They make a **square corner** where they cross. Perpendicular line segments form square corners, too.

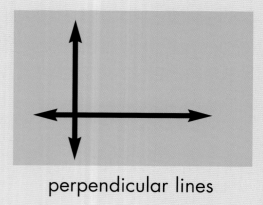

perpendicular lines

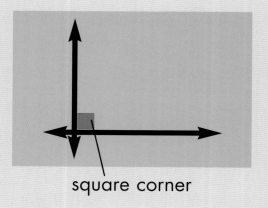

square corner

Activity Box

Put both arms straight up in the air. They look like parallel lines. Now, put one arm straight up. Point the other arm straight out to the side. What kind of lines do your arms make now?

Perpendicular lines

Can you find perpendicular lines?
Can you find parallel lines?

Angles

The ferris wheel has rays.
The ride also has **angles**.

An angle is made up of two rays
or two line segments. The two rays
or line segments have the same
endpoint. That endpoint is called
the **vertex** of the angle.

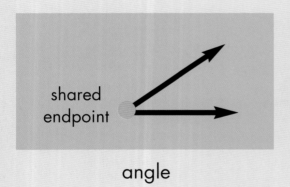

shared
endpoint

angle

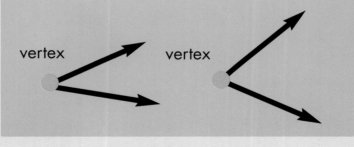

vertex   vertex

angles of different sizes

Activity Box

14

Make different size angles with your hand.

A ferris wheel shows many angles of many sizes.

Aunt Sarah holds her hand out to show angles with openings of different sizes.

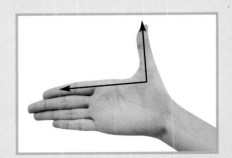

Different Angles

Angles have special names too,
just as pairs of lines do.

There are **right angles**. Right angles
are angles that make a square corner.
Perpendicular lines form the square corner.

There are **acute angles**. Any angle
with an opening smaller than a right
angle is an acute angle.

There are **obtuse angles**. Any angle
with an opening greater than a right
angle is an obtuse angle.

Activity Box

Use your arms to make each kind of angle.
Show a small opening for an acute angle.
Show a great big opening for an obtuse
angle. Then draw each kind of angle on paper.

Find the right angles, acute angles, and obtuse angles.

The Last Ride

Aunt Sarah agrees to take the children on one last ride. While they wait, they talk about the geometry they see around them.

Ethan sees points and line segments.

Grace sees parallel and perpendicular line segments.

Aunt Sarah sees different angles.

They all see intersecting line segments.

What do you see?

Activity Box

How many different kinds of lines and angles can you find in the picture?

Angles and lines
are everywhere.

Geometry Around Us

Grace and Ethan leave the fair tired, but happy. The children learned a lot about geometry. See what you learned in this book by answering the questions below.

How are a line and a line segment different?

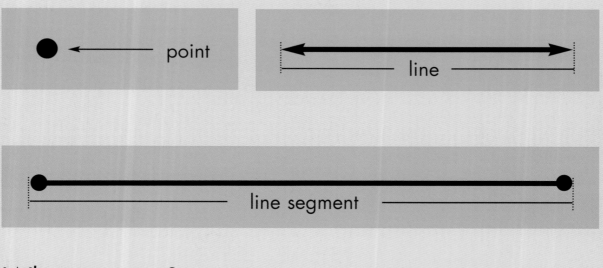

What is a ray?

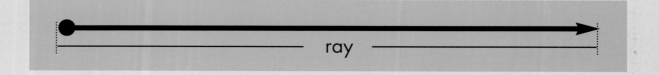

Where might you see parallel lines and perpendicular lines?

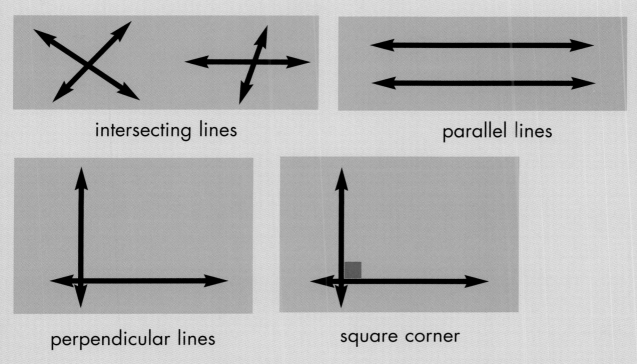

intersecting lines

parallel lines

perpendicular lines

square corner

Can you name different kinds of angles? You can use the glossary and index on the following pages to find the names of these angles.

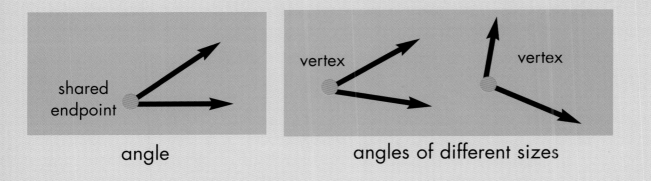

shared endpoint

angle

vertex

vertex

angles of different sizes

Now that you know the basics, you can see geometry wherever you go!

Glossary

acute angle An angle with an opening smaller than a right angle

angles A figure formed by two rays or line segments that share an endpoint

endpoint An exact location showing the end of a line segment or the end of a ray

geometry A study of points, lines, angles, and shapes

intersecting Crossing at some point

line A straight path extending in both directions with no endpoints

line segment Part of a line that includes two endpoints

obtuse angle An angle with an opening greater than a right angle

parallel Never crossing and always the same distance apart

perpendicular Lines or line segments that intersect to form right angles with a square corner

point An exact position or location

ray A part of a line that continues on in one direction from an endpoint

right angle An angle that forms a square corner

square corner A corner that looks like part of a square, such as the corner of a door or a book

vertex The point where two or more line segments or rays meet

Index